A DAY THAT MADE HISTORY

3rd September, 1939

Sheila Gordon

Dryad Press Limited   London

Contents

THE EVENTS

THE INVESTIGATION

Acknowledgments

The author and publishers wish to thank the following for their kind permission to reproduce copyright illustrations: Imperial War Museum, pages 6, 10, 22, 23, 26, 39, 40, 42, 43, 44, 45, 47, 51, 59, 60; Topham Picture Library, pages 11, 12, 17, 20, 21, 32, 36, 37, 38, 52; The Wiener Library, pages 34, 48, 49, 58.

The "Day that Made History" series was devised by Nathaniel Harris.

All rights reserved. No part of this publication may be reproduced, in any form or by any means, without permission from the publishers.

© Sheila Gordon 1988. First published 1988.

Typeset by Tek-Art Ltd, Kent, and printed and bound by Richard Clay Ltd, Chichester, Sussex for the publishers, Dryad Press Limited, 8 Cavendish Square, London W1M 0AJ

ISBN 0 8521 9757 8

THE
EVENTS

Prologue to a war

Thursday, 31st August, 1939 – the end of a holiday season in Europe that had been fraught with anxiety and tension as the diplomatic crisis deepened.

Adolf Hitler, the German Chancellor, was constantly making speeches calling for peace, but at the same time he was keeping up his relentless pressure on the neighbouring country of Poland, insisting that she should allow the port of Danzig to be returned to Germany. Danzig had once been a German port, but at the end of the First World War had been taken away from Germany and made an independent city under the jurisdiction of the League of Nations, though remaining within the Polish customs area. This had been a severe blow to German pride, and now, twenty years later, Hitler was determined to get Danzig back.

Since Hitler's rise to power in 1933, no one either in his own country or in the rest of Europe had managed to frustrate his plans for long, and once again he was determined to get his way – if not by bullying and threats, then by force.

The Poles refused even to consider the matter. Britain and France, who had both signed agreements which bound them to defend Poland if she were invaded, were being urged by Hitler to exert a moderating influence on their intransigent ally. But so far the constant meetings, telephone calls, telegrams and flights between Berlin, London, Paris and Warsaw had achieved nothing.

The generals of the German High Command, many of whom disliked and mistrusted Hitler, were thoroughly confused by his alternating promises of peace and threats of war. They pressed for a firm decision, and by 12.30 p.m. on 31st August Hitler had decided that he could not keep them waiting any longer. He signed "Directive No. 1 for the Conduct of the War", and at 4 o'clock that afternoon the High

Command of the *Wehrmacht*, the German armed forces, ordered the invasion of Poland to take place the following morning.

Throughout the night of 31st August and the early hours of 1st September tanks, guns, lorries and half a million men moved towards the Polish border. At 4.45 a.m. the orders to invade took effect and the German guns opened fire. At 6 a.m. planes of the German air force – the *Luftwaffe* – started to bomb Warsaw and other Polish cities.

Shortly before 10 a.m., in Berlin, Hitler began his drive to the Kroll Opera House to address the German Parliament, the *Reichstag*, whose usual meeting place, the *Reichstag* building, had been destroyed by fire in 1933. There was no sign of the admiring crowds who usually applauded Hitler's drives through the city. Reports of hostilities had begun to be broadcast on German radio, but the cheers and flags that had greeted the news of his invasion of Austria in 1938 were absent on this occasion. The attitude of the German public seemed tense and apprehensive.

In London a picture of events was slowly pieced together as reports filtered through. The first that the British Foreign Secretary, Lord Halifax, knew of what was happening in Poland was when he received a transcript of Hitler's proclamation to his army, which had been broadcast on Berlin radio. Then came a single telegram from Warsaw, reporting the first German air-raids, and this was quickly followed by an urgent demand from the Polish ambassador in London, Count Racynski, to see Halifax immediately. He had little new information to add, but he confirmed that Warsaw had been bombed and told Halifax that the Polish frontier had been crossed by the German army at four points.

Halifax immediately summoned Theo Kordt, the German chargé d'affaires, to No. 10 Downing Street, where they talked in a small downstairs office. Halifax relayed the news to Kordt, who declared himself completely ignorant of what was going on, and went back to his embassy to see what further information he could get from the radio.

A cabinet meeting had already been arranged for 10.30 a.m. and Halifax went immediately to see the Prime Minister, Neville Chamberlain, to acquaint him with the situation and to discuss the possible courses of action to be suggested to the cabinet ministers.

It was a sober meeting. The American ambassador had by then passed on to Halifax more reports of German ground and air attacks, and it seemed clear to the whole cabinet that

Britain now had no choice but to come to the aid of her ally.

Chamberlain, who had spent the previous two years trying to reach an understanding with Hitler, reluctantly agreed. Nevertheless, even at this stage, there still lingered the desperate hope that Hitler might change his mind, and present a proposal that could be honourably accepted. There was also another important factor to consider: the need for coordination and cooperation with the French government.

The cabinet decided to draw up the draft of an official communication to be sent to Germany, making quite clear the British government's intention of honouring the treaty obligations to Poland. The ministers were also determined that Hitler should be given a time limit within which he must withdraw his troops. They wanted no chance of days being wasted in discussion while Poland was being overrun by German forces. They felt reasonably reassured by Chamberlain's apparently firm attitude, by the knowledge that the British armed forces were already being mobilized and that contingents of the army and air force on their way to France. They were confident that the French would agree with their draft communiqué, and that exact details of the time limit could safely be left for Chamberlain and Halifax to settle with the French.

However, the French Council of Ministers meeting in Paris at the same time took a different view. Although mobilization had been ordered, Georges Bonnet, the French Foreign Minister, insisted that nothing in the nature of a time limit must be imposed before the French parliament had approved the war budget – and Parliament was not due to meet until 3 o'clock that afternoon.

Halifax and Chamberlain decided that they must wait – but their patience was to bring them no reward; even after the budget had been authorized, Bonnet still refused to specify a time limit to Hitler. He regarded it as too early to issue such a clear ultimatum and preferred to move much more cautiously than Chamberlain and Halifax wished.

Bonnet's attitude put Chamberlain in a difficult position with the British Parliament. Many M.P.s on both sides of the House of Commons were suspicious of the Prime Minister, because of his past record of appeasement – making concessions to Hitler in the hope of pacifying him. Such M.P.s feared that, faced with Hitler's latest threats, Chamberlain might once again back down. His address to the Commons at 6 p.m. sounded firm enough, but there were many complaints about the absence of a time limit in the official British message to be sent to Hitler. Chamberlain reiterated his determination to stand by the guarantees to Poland, and assured the Members of Parliament that if Hitler failed to give a satisfactory reply, the British ambassador in Berlin would be instructed to ask for his passport and return home – the traditional diplomatic method of informing another country that war was inevitable and imminent.

At 7.15 p.m. the British ambassador in Berlin, Sir Nevile Henderson, presented himself with the communiqué to Ribbentrop, the German Foreign Minister, who received him courteously and tried to start a discussion about the rights and wrongs of the Polish position. Henderson refused to be drawn in, but told Ribbentrop that he would be ready at any time to receive the German reply. He was immediately followed by the French ambassador, who handed over an identical communication. No mention was made of a time limit.

By the morning of 2nd September there had been no reply, and the war in Poland was increasing in ferocity. The largely unmechanized and traditionally trained Polish forces had been no match for the highly mechanized German army whose soldiers were drilled in the latest techniques of modern warfare. They were now penetrating deep into Polish territory, supported by intensified bombing of Polish cities and railway networks by the *Luftwaffe*.

Crowds gathered in Downing Street as the crisis deepened. They waved their encouragement to the cabinet ministers and M.P.s as they arrived.

In London tension continued to rise. Crowds had been forming outside 10 Downing Street and the Houses of Parliament since early morning. The people, though apparently calm, even cheerful, were confused and uncertain. The Members of Parliament, who at this stage had no inkling of Chamberlain's protracted negotiations with the French, were as puzzled as the crowds watching them arrive at the House of Commons. They were growing increasingly suspicious of Chamberlain's intentions.

By the afternoon Bonnet had in fact declared himself willing to impose a time limit, but he was still insisting that it must be at least forty-eight hours, so that France could complete a full mobilization before war started. Chamberlain and Halifax were aghast at this news. They knew they needed to cooperate with the French, but they were also aware of their greater need of the support of their own Parliament, which would inevitably be critical of further delay.

Then came a further complication. Count Ciano, the Italian Foreign Minister, telephoned to announce that the Italian government, which had strong and friendly ties with Germany, was now prepared to take a hand in the crisis. With French approval, Ciano had suggested an armistice to Hitler; this could then be followed by a five-power conference to settle the dispute between Germany and Poland. Hitler, who had done very well out of the four-power conference on Czechoslovakia the previous year, had asked for twenty-four hours to consider the proposal. France was prepared to agree. How about Britain?

When informed of this new proposal, the British cabinet was adamant that it should be refused. The ministers responsible for the armed services pointed out that any further delay would put Britain at risk from surprise air attack – and moreover they were all embarrassingly aware of the increasingly desperate appeals for help from Poland.

Once again the cabinet ministers left the meeting convinced that their clear line of policy had been accepted. Once again they were to find their view discounted in favour of the further delay urged by the French. When they took their seats on the front bench of the House of Commons that evening, they expected to hear the Prime Minister expounding the stern message they had recommended, and warning that war was now almost inevitable. To their horror, Chamberlain, still trying to stay in line with the French, talked mainly of Ciano's proposals and Britain's desire for peace.

This was not what the members of the cabinet or the rest of

the Commons had come to hear, and Chamberlain found himself with all parties ranged against him. When Arthur Greenwood, the deputy leader of the Labour Party, got up to speak, the Conservative Leo Amery's cry of "Speak for England, Arthur!" was taken up from both sides of the House with shouts of "Speak for Britain! Speak for the working classes!" It was therefore Greenwood, a member of the Opposition, rather than the Prime Minister, who made the firm and resolute speech that the House of Commons wanted to hear.

Furious, the members of the cabinet departed from the Chamber to hold an impromptu meeting in a nearby room. They decided to confront the Prime Minister with their displeasure immediately. Chamberlain accepted Halifax's warning that he had no choice but to listen to them. At such a critical time he could not afford any possibility of his ministers' resigning from the cabinet. Chamberlain decided to put the wishes of Parliament before those of the French government and service chiefs. His painstaking efforts to maintain Franco-British unity were abandoned, and he agreed that the British ultimatum would be sent as originally planned.

As the day drew to an end, the ministers made their way to Downing Street through a heavy thunderstorm, for a last peace-time cabinet meeting. The moment for decisive action had come and this time there could be no turning back.

3rd September: "Right gentlemen, this means war"

The midnight chimes of Big Ben tolled just as usual over a "blacked out" London. Since 1st September the street lighting that could have proved invaluable to enemy aircraft had been switched off, and people were getting used to walking and driving through darkened streets.

At the cabinet meeting, begun half an hour before, Chamberlain was "calm, even icy cold", according to Sir Reginald Dorman Smith, the Minister for Agriculture. He accepted without question the timetable for procedure that was now thrashed out.

Everyone agreed that the time for patient diplomacy was over; Britain must now act without France. Immediate instructions must be sent to Sir Nevile Henderson in Berlin, ordering him to see Ribbentrop at 9 a.m. He was to say that a state of war would exist between Britain and Germany, unless Hitler sent a favourable reply to the original British communication by 11 o'clock that morning.

The Prime Ministers of the Dominions (the self-governing territories of the British Commonwealth) were to be informed of the ultimatum at 9 a.m., and Parliament would be told at noon.

Dorman Smith remembers Chamberlain saying quietly at the end of the meeting: "Right gentlemen, this means war" – words immediately followed by an enormous thunderclap and a flash of lightning that lit up the cabinet room.

Halifax, who went on to the Foreign Office to arrange the telegram to Henderson, sat for a while with his staff drinking beer. He looked relieved that the decision had at last been taken. Then he, like the rest of the cabinet, went home to rest and to wait.

Broadcasting time had already been reserved provisionally for the Prime Minister. At ten past eleven in the morning it was certain that no reply had come from Germany, and Chamberlain began his broadcast five minutes later, looking, as one BBC official later recalled, "tired, crumpled and old".

Minutes after the broadcast had ended, the wail of air-raid sirens sent Londoners running for the nearest cover they could find. But after fifteen minutes the "all clear" was sounded, and they emerged, thankful that the devastation they had seen on newsreels of the Spanish Civil War had not happened to them – yet. They were not informed that it had all been a mistake – that a stray French aircraft approaching Dover had been mistaken for an enemy plane. Nor were they told that the two British fighter planes sent to intercept it had collided over the Thames, causing the first death of the war.

The House of Commons assembled at noon. There was a strange atmosphere, for not only was it the first Parliament of the war – it was also the first time Parliament had met on a Sunday for 120 years. Despite the odd and disturbing circumstances, the usual Speaker's procession and, in Churchill's words, "brief stately prayers" began the proceedings.

Chamberlain repeated to a tense House the news he had already broadcast to the British people. It was a bitter moment for him. Many of the M.P.s present had criticized his policies and labelled him an appeaser of both Hitler and Mussolini, Hitler's ally and fellow dictator. Now they had got what they wanted and Britain was at war – at that moment alone, for the French ultimatum had only just been handed in, and would not expire until 5 o'clock that evening. For many of those who were listening to Chamberlain there was a sense of relief that the waiting was over, and that a determined and honourable stand had been made. Chamberlain did not share

Running for shelter as the siren sounds.

their feelings. He had tried to avoid a war that he knew would bring to Europe, perhaps to the world, unimaginable suffering and destruction. It was with deep personal feeling that he told his audience: "Everything I have worked for, everything that I have believed in during my public life, has crashed in ruins." Chamberlain left the Commons as soon as he had finished speaking.

Winston Churchill, who for the past ten years had been warning the country of the danger from Germany, sat in his place on the Conservative back benches, wondering whether he would now be given a part to play. Soon after he had taken his seat, he received a summons from Chamberlain that was

Neville Chamberlain leaving 10 Downing Street on his way to the House of Commons.

to bring to an end his long exclusion from the centre stage of politics. Chamberlain offered him the key post of First Lord of the Admiralty in succession to Earl Stanhope, and Churchill was delighted to accept. Not only did it bring him immediately into the heart of the action, but it was an office that he had held before, during the First World War, until he had been forced to leave after the failure of one of his schemes, the naval expedition to the Dardanelles.

He knew from his early experience that the conduct of war cannot be regulated by a normal timetable, and that he could not afford to wait for his formal appointment by the King on

Winston Churchill arriving at Downing Street.

5th September before starting work. He must take charge of the war at sea immediately. He sent a message straight away to the Admiralty, informing them that he was taking over at once and that they could expect him at six o'clock that evening. This evoked a delighted response and a signal went out to all ships of the Fleet: "Winston is back!"

So it came about that Churchill, now aged sixty-four, found himself sitting in the same chair at the same desk that he had left twenty-five years before, with the map case he had installed then still fixed on the wall behind him.

He knew that in terms of sea power the outlook for Britain was reasonably good, because the German navy had only recently begun to be rebuilt. He did, however, greatly underestimate the part that submarines were going to play in modern war. In fact, from the minute war broke out, German U-boats, already posted in the western approaches to Britain, would begin their hunt for British and French shipping.

Meanwhile the House of Commons had also been busy. The National Service (Armed Forces) Bill had been hurried through all its stages, to ensure that the conscription to the armed forces of all men who were fit, and not working in jobs of crucial importance to the war effort, was as speedy as possible.

Chamberlain, who had returned to 10 Downing Street after seeing Churchill, spent the rest of the afternoon forming his War Cabinet, the inner circle of nine men who were to be responsible for the overall conduct of the war.

At 5 p.m., just at the time that France's declaration of war was taking effect, these nine men met together for the first time. They were Chamberlain himself, Lord Halifax, Sir John Simon, Sir Samuel Hoare, Lord Chatfield, Lord Hankey, Leslie Hore-Belisha, Kingsley Wood and Winston Churchill. They appointed Lord Gort as Commander-in-Chief of the British Expeditionary Force in France, and Lord Ironside as Chief of the Imperial General Staff – the military head of all the armed forces in the Commonwealth.

By 7.30 p.m. the War Minister, Leslie Hore-Belisha, was meeting with King George VI at Buckingham Palace to inform him of the recommendations of the War Cabinet. He had been told not to bother to wear the usual morning coat and top hat – a small but significant sign of the relaxation in formality that the demands of wartime were to bring. The King and Queen had returned to the Palace earlier that week, as soon as they had received reports of the worsening crisis.

They had left the two young princesses at Balmoral, where they were to remain for safety until December.

The King's diaries and letters make no secret of his own longing for peace or of his sympathy and support for Chamberlain. He had himself seen active service in the First World War and was under no illusions about the human suffering that would result from a second one. He now found himself burdened not only with the Crown, as a result of his brother's abdication in 1937, but also with the formidable task of providing a focus and symbol for a nation and Common-wealth at war. His constitutional position prevented him from playing an executive role, but it was his duty to be informed of every detail of his ministers' policies and to bear the anxieties that inevitably accompanied that responsibility.

His first wartime broadcast was made that night – an ordeal for him as always, because of his speech impediment, which he carefully controlled, as well as for many of his listeners whose own anxieties were sharpened by his slow, strained delivery. Nevertheless, on this occasion, the frequent long pauses served only to intensify the obvious depth of his feeling as he concluded:

"There may be dark days ahead, and war can no longer be confined to the battlefield. But we can only do the right as we see the right, and reverently commit our cause to God. If one and all we keep resolutely faithful to it, ready for whatever service or sacrifice it may demand, then with God's help we shall prevail."

The speech struck a sombre note. And before the day was out both King and people were to receive sombre news of the first wartime disaster at sea. The passenger liner *Athenia*, bound for New York, had been torpedoed by a German U-boat, whose commander claimed that he had mistaken it for an armed merchant ship. 112 passengers were drowned, 28 of whom were American citizens. It was a tragic foreshadowing of the terrible casualties at sea that were to come.

Fortunately for the apprehensive British and French peoples, there were no corresponding events on land or in the air. 3rd September, like the six months of "phoney war" that were to follow, was distinguished by peaceful skies and the absence of any engagement with the enemy.

Hitler asks: "What now?"

The series of telegrams sent to Germany from London in the early hours of 3rd September kept the British ambassador, Sir Nevile Henderson, and his staff on tenterhooks.

The first one, warning them to be ready for further important instructions, was received shortly after midnight. Thirty-five minutes later came the second message: "You should ask for an appointment with the M.F.A. [Minister for Foreign Affairs] at 9 a.m. on Sunday morning. Instructions will follow." Then at 4 a.m. the final message arrived, confirming the instructions for a meeting, and giving the text of the note to be handed to Ribbentrop.

But in those early hours of a Sunday morning it was not so easy to get hold of the German Foreign Minister. Henderson was firmly told that Ribbentrop was "unavailable", and that the communication from Britain must be left with his official interpreter, Doctor Paul Schmidt. Sir Nevile duly arrived at the Foreign Office in the Wilhelmstrasse, promptly at 9 a.m., carrying his historic message; he had no suspicion that Schmidt himself had only just managed to get there in time to receive him. He had overslept and had rushed to the meeting in a hastily ordered taxi.

Schmidt recalls in his memoirs that Henderson entered the room looking "very serious". He refused to sit down and stood in the middle of the room to read his message. It reminded the German government of the note already sent on 2nd September and pointed out that not only had no answer been forthcoming but that the attacks on Poland had been intensified. Accordingly, unless assurances were received from the German government by 11 o'clock that morning, a state of war would exist between Britain and Germany from that hour.

The two men, who were personal friends, then shook hands, and Henderson returned to the Embassy to arrange the removal of his personal belongings to the Hotel Adlon, and his eventual return to London.

Schmidt rushed over to the Chancellery, where he had to push through a small crowd of members of the German cabinet and high-ranking party officials who were anxiously awaiting news. As he entered the *Führer*'s office, Schmidt saw that there were two men in the room – Hitler, sitting at his desk, and the "unavailable" von Ribbentrop standing at the window. They looked up expectantly and Schmidt's careful translation of the British ultimatum was received in complete silence. For a space of time that Schmidt found interminable, Hitler sat still, gazing into space. Then, with a "savage look", he turned to Ribbentrop, who remained at the window, and demanded: "What now?" His tone seemed to Schmidt to imply that he had been misled by Ribbentrop's false estimate of Britain's mood – but Ribbentrop remained impassive, merely replying: "I assume that the French will hand in a similar ultimatum within the hour."

Schmidt left to inform the waiting crowd in the anteroom that war was imminent. For a moment there was silence. Then Reichsmarshall Goering, the head of the *Luftwaffe*, turned to Schmidt with the words: "If we lose this war, then God help us." Goebbels, the Minister of Propaganda, said nothing. "Everywhere in the room," Schmidt recalls, "there were looks of grave concern."

Amid the atmosphere of gloomy resignation, there was still one person in Berlin trying, even in these last hours of peace, to hold back the tide of war. This was Birger Dahlerus, a Swedish friend of Goering, who since August had been trying to convince his German friends that this time the British were determined to stand firm. As soon as he now heard of the British ultimatum, he urged Goering to persuade Hitler to send a conciliatory reply, and said he personally was ready to fly to Britain at a moment's notice to negotiate a settlement on Germany's behalf. He claims in his account of the period that Hitler seemed interested, but there is no German confirmation of this. In any case, his desperate telephone calls to Britain about his proposed dash by aeroplane met with a curt and dismissive response from Halifax, who would no longer risk becoming enmeshed in false hopes of German cooperation. Dahlerus was to admit years later that he had totally misjudged German intentions, and had been far too quick to believe their protestations of goodwill. His story is an interesting illustration of the passionate desire for peace which led so many Europeans into a naive and over-optimistic assessment of German policy.

Now the time of uncertainty was over. The world was to be left in no doubt of the German attitude. Shortly after 11 a.m. Ribbentrop sent for Henderson and handed over the German reply to the British ultimatum. It contained an outright refusal of British demands, and a long statement accusing Britain of "preaching the destruction and extermination of the German people".

An eyewitness account recalls the clear, sunny autumn

Sir Nevile Henderson returning home.

weather of that morning, and the sudden unheralded announcements over the loudspeakers in the Wilhelmstrasse that Great Britain had declared war on Germany. Some 250 people stood listening silently. Newsboys quickly appeared on the scene selling hastily printed "extras" with their headlines: "BRITISH ULTIMATUM TURNED DOWN", "ENGLAND DECLARES A STATE OF WAR" and "GERMAN MEMORANDUM PROVES ENGLAND's GUILT".

So far Britain alone was presented as the villain of the piece. France had not, as Ribbentrop had predicted, declared war within the hour, as she was still impeded by disagreements within the French cabinet. However, by the early hours of Sunday morning, even the hopeful Foreign Minister Bonnet had to accept that Mussolini's last-ditch intervention had come to nothing, and Prime Minister Daladier managed at last to persuade the French generals that they could manage with less delay. Eventually a message was wired through to the French ambassador in Berlin with instructions to give Ribbentrop an ultimatum expiring at 5 o'clock that afternoon.

Ribbentrop tried to persuade the ambassador, Robert Coulondre, that Germany was reluctant to attack France and that she genuinely wished to agree to Mussolini's proposals. It was to no avail. Coulondre stuck firmly to the prepared French position and emphasized the heavy responsibility that Germany must bear.

Whatever Hitler's anxieties about the day's events, in one area at least he felt confident. The news from the Polish front was excellent, and his troops – commanded by generals who were, for the only time in the war, untroubled by Hitler's interference – had penetrated 50 miles into Polish territory.

Hitler decided to travel immediately to general head-quarters in Eastern Germany, but before joining his special train, he attended to several important matters of policy. He issued his second war directive, ordering that all efforts be concentrated on a speedy victory over Poland; there was to be no attack on Britain and France except at sea. No air strikes were to be mounted unless Germany was hit first, and even then only if "prospects of success were particularly favourable". The directive went on to order that the whole of German industrial production was to be geared to the success of the war effort.

Next came a letter to Mussolini. Hitler had been disappointed by Italy's decision to remain neutral, but he was determined, nevertheless, to make sure of Italian friendship and diplomatic support. His letter spoke of his gratitude to the *Duce* for his attempts at mediation, and explained that his decision to let the war go ahead was based on his fear that further delay would have allowed France and Britain to increase their military strength to a dangerous level.

He then turned his attention to securing more firmly the non-aggression pact recently negotiated with Soviet Russia. Since the very beginning of the German invasion of Poland, the Russians had been helping German pilots by continually sending out signals from the Soviet radio station at Minsk. These signals enabled the pilots of German bombers to confirm their position accurately and to navigate an exact route to Polish cities. The Russians had even gone so far as to keep the station operating two hours after the usual time in order to assist night attacks. Hitler was greatly encouraged by the news of this Soviet cooperation, which reached him on 3rd September. He immediately sent a message to Stalin, the Russian leader, inviting him to join Germany in the invasion of Poland; Russia would have the chance to grab land from Poland, in return for providing military reinforcement for the German forces. Hitler hoped that this arrangement would also ensure continuing Russian friendship, even after the Poles had been finally beaten.

So, ironically, Hitler embarked on a war which his policies had precipitated, supported by a country to whose political organization he had always been fiercely opposed. The Russians, in their eagerness to cooperate, did not foresee that their country, in its turn, would be suddenly and savagely invaded by German forces, nor that they would ultimately inflict a crushing defeat on their former accomplice.

The home front in Britain

While the politicians and diplomats were busy with their meetings and arrangements, ordinary British people got on with their first wartime Sunday.

Many of them had been disturbed in the early hours by thunderstorms that had persisted until about 2 a.m., but they eventually woke to clear skies and warm sunshine. They no longer had any means of finding out how long the good weather was likely to last, because the Meteorological Office's forecast of "Showers, bright intervals, local thunderstorms, rather warm" was not issued either to the newspapers or to the B.B.C. Strict censorship had already been imposed even before official hostilities had started, and weather forecasts would not be heard or read again until the end of the war. They were considered to be of too much potential value to the German air force.

The Sunday newspapers carried long reports of the savage fighting in Poland, and the two-hourly news bulletins from the B.B.C. confirmed that the German advance was continuing. The situation still seemed ominous.

Anyone wanting to switch to something more cheerful on the radio was disappointed. The B.B.C., already established in its wartime headquarters in the country, had reduced its normal eight regional programmes to just one – the Home Service – and as yet this could offer little variety. The news broadcasts were interspersed mainly with light music played by Sandy Macpherson on his cinema organ. However, avid listeners to the news at least had the pleasure of being able to tune in at 6, instead of the hitherto prescribed time of 10 a.m.

Churches and chapels were well attended that morning and radios had been brought in to most of them so that the congregation could listen to the Prime Minister's 11.15 a.m. broadcast. Many clergymen had two sermons ready, so that they would be equipped with the appropriate response to either peace or war.

The wail of the air-raid sirens which sounded over London and the Home Counties as soon as the fateful broadcast was over provoked a variety of responses. Some church services continued, while others ended prematurely as ministers advised their congregations to return to their homes as quickly as possible. Some of those not in church carried on with their cooking, but many more hurried to take cover under staircases, in cellars or in Anderson shelters at the bottom of their gardens. £42,000,000 had already been spent by the government on supplying these shelters to families who wished to install them. They were delivered as separate sheets of thick corrugated iron which had to be bolted together. The shelter was then sunk into a deep trench and covered with soil and sandbags. The simple structures gave no protection against a direct hit from a bomb, but they were to prove effective shelters against bomb blast and the dangerous debris that flew about after an explosion.

Mrs. M.I. Cottrell, who had no Anderson shelter, talked later about her experiences and remembered how her husband reacted to the sound of that first air-raid warning. He rushed round the house nailing blankets over doors and windows and stuffing the oven cloth up the chimney to ensure that the house was insulated from the effects of a gas attack. He made sure that there would be no danger from flying glass by sticking two-inch tape in a criss-cross pattern on all the windows, so that even if shattered by an explosion they would not fly through the air in lethal fragments, but would fall neatly on the ground in large pieces. He also remembered to fill the bath with water in case the house should be struck by incendiaries – small bombs designed to burst into flame on impact, but which could be extinguished if dealt with promptly.

Mr Cottrell was particularly careful and well-informed because he was one of the two million people who had

Many homes and businesses were hidden behind sandbags to protect them against bomb blast.

A soldier on the way to join his unit.

volunteered for the civil defence services and had already been thoroughly educated about the dangers of air-raids and about the precautions that could be taken to minimize casualties.

Now the news of the outbreak of war sent many more men and women to their nearest civil defence headquarters to offer their services – and there was also a great increase, even in this one day, of applicants wishing to join the army, navy and air force without waiting for their official call-up. In London, the recruiting office in New Scotland Yard was kept open even though it was Sunday, and it was besieged by thousands of people eager to become members of the armed forces.

Those who in the preceding months had joined the territorial army – the voluntary spare-time force that kept trained in readiness for war – were already on their way to join their units. Young men in the 20-year-old age-group, who had already been called up, could be seen wandering aimlessly round the towns in which they were stationed. A housewife in Portsmouth recorded in her diary having watched with some sadness hundreds of newly conscripted naval ratings "wandering up and down the streets with a slightly brooding far-away look on their faces". Certainly, in that cinema-going period, most people, including the young, had had plenty of opportunity to see newsreels of the Spanish Civil War and of the Japanese attack on China, and so few of the young servicemen could have been unaware of the horrors that war might inflict on them.

Evacuees, too, were still on the move on 3rd September. Railways and local authorities were working to complete the enormous task of moving over a million schoolchildren, as well as infants with their mothers, away from the danger areas to the many counties in Britain that were safely out of the range of German bombers. The railway companies were congratulated from all sides for their success in handling such a massive exodus. It was reported that some main line stations were coping with evacuees throughout the twenty-four hours of the day.

There were some tearful scenes, but many eye-witnesses described reasonably cheerful children marching in twos to their trains. Gas masks in cardboard boxes were slung round their necks and they carried haversacks and shoebags bulging with precious possessions.

There are many descriptions of the scenes later in the day when the children arrived at their destinations. Harassed billeting officers trying to allot the children to suitable families were often pushed aside by prospective foster parents who, alarmed by reports of the poor condition that some of the children were in, moved about the rows of evacuees waiting on village greens and in church halls and picked out those who looked the cleanest and most attractive. The memories of those children and adults who were left unchosen at the end of the day make painful reading. "We were just like cattle," wrote one evacuee mother, and though many welcomed the escape to safety and, in some cases, to greatly improved living conditions, there were others who found the adjustment too difficult and in a few weeks returned home thankfully, even to bad housing and the risk of bombs.

Human beings were not the only evacuees that day. Rare animals including two giant pandas were transported from the

Evacuees on their way to safety, 3rd September, 1939.

London Zoo to Whipsnade; the age-old Coronation Chair was removed from Westminster Abbey to safe storage in the country; and the most valuable paintings in the National Gallery were carefully packed up and moved to deep slate quarries in the Welsh Mountains.

In London, once the scare from the sirens was over, thousands of people flocked to the West End. There were crowds outside Downing Street and the Houses of Parliament all the time, waving and calling encouragement to the ministers who came and went during an increasingly busy day. Photographs convey a surprisingly cheerful atmosphere and many people who waited there remember their feelings of pride and relief that the government was standing firm and that at last the time of uncertainty was over.

London's parks were full of sunbathers, and restaurants found no difficulty in filling their tables. One eye-witness who had to drive along the Edgware Road during the middle of the day recalls his surprise at the holiday mood. "Outside every pub and place of amusement there were swarms of people drinking on the pavements, many drunk, singing lustily and dancing."

There was no public entertainment available because theatres, cinemas, music halls and dance halls had been temporarily shut down until adequate shelters could be provided nearby. Concert parties travelling across Britain to their new bookings found themselves stranded as piers and music halls were suddenly closed. Fortunately for them, and for a public in search of distraction from wartime worries, this was only a short-term deprivation and entertainment started

Gas masks had been issued, specially fitted to people of all ages.

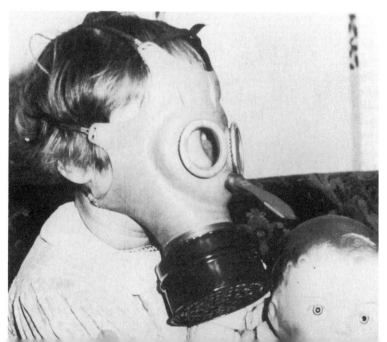

up again after two or three weeks. Films like *Bachelor Mother*, starring David Niven and Ginger Rogers, and musicals like *Me and My Girl* opened up to their usual enthusiastic audiences; dance halls proved more popular than ever, especially for the servicemen and women away from home and in need of a change from barrack-room life.

The 200,000 people who owned television sets did not receive any Sunday entertainment from the B.B.C. All television transmissions were discontinued without warning and the screens remained blank until after the end of the war.

The King's radio broadcast that night proved to be a major focus for the whole country and most people made sure that they switched on again for the 9 o'clock news, preceded as always by the chimes of Big Ben.

Outside, wardens patrolled the streets making sure that all black-out arrangements were effective and that the whole of Britain was in darkness. Anyone venturing out had to rely on the beams of a torch which even then had to be carefully used and kept firmly pointed towards the ground.

People taking a last look at the Sunday newspapers before going to bed were reminded not only of the fighting in Poland but also of all the new regulations about matters such as rationing, identity cards, gas masks, and national service, that were to result in a transformation of their daily life.

Even so, the newspapers reminded them, too, that even in wartime many things remained unchanged. There were still houses for sale, jobs available, Christmas bulbs to be ordered, and "early autumn frocks" to be bought for six and a half guineas, "likely to prove useful to busy women at this present time".

They were also reminded, perhaps, as they read the agricultural reports, that any country engaged in war has to make sure of its food supplies. Whatever else had been happening on that day of 3rd September, the news was that the farmers of Britain were out in their fields, and that although they were somewhat worried by the early morning mists, which made it difficult to dry off the stooks of corn (combine harvesters were as yet not in general use), nevertheless the harvest of 1939 was almost completely gathered in.

THE INVESTIGATION

What were the roots of the problem?

We have seen how the disagreement between Germany and Poland exploded into violent conflict. This started off a chain reaction engulfing first Britain and France, and ultimately most of the world. Our concern now is to investigate the origins of that explosion – to discover how events in twentieth-century Europe had created such a critical situation.

The background Disputes about territorial boundaries have always been a major feature of European history. It could hardly be otherwise in an area where so many different nationalities are contained in one land mass. The ease of communication between one European country and another has facilitated trade and development; but it has also meant that it has been equally easy to wage war.

By the beginning of the twentieth century, the traditional sources of European conflict had been extended by new quarrels about colonies, naval power and the rights of small nations to govern themselves.

Germany, originally a collection of separate states under the domination of Prussia, was now a politically and geographically unified nation with one federal government and under the rule of one sovereign – Kaiser Wilhelm II. He was determined to win influence and power for his nation both in Europe and in Africa, and to ensure that she enjoyed unrivalled military, naval and economic pre-eminence. His aggressive policies and his alliance with Austria-Hungary were regarded with great suspicion by other European nations equally anxious to lead the world and eventually provoked an opposing alliance between Britain, France and Russia. The intensifying hostility between the two blocs, their formidable military capability and the frequent clashes of interest led eventually to the Great War of 1914-18, now known as the First World War.

Versailles   That war ended with the defeat of Germany and her Austrian ally. In 1919 the victorious powers (who by the end of the war included Great Britain, France, Italy, Japan and the United States) met in the Palace of Versailles, near Paris, to draw up a peace settlement. There were two conflicting motives underlying their decisions: the wish to provide a new political and geographical framework that would ensure a peaceful and prosperous Europe, and the desire to punish Germany.

Whatever the arguments caused by the tension between the desire for peace and the desire for revenge, on one point all could agree: Germany must never again be allowed to threaten the peace of Europe – her power must be reduced and limited once and for all.

The final settlement left Germany furious and resentful about specific areas on the map of Europe, which had been redrawn to her disadvantage.

The Versailles conference in the Hall of Mirrors in the Palace of Versailles.

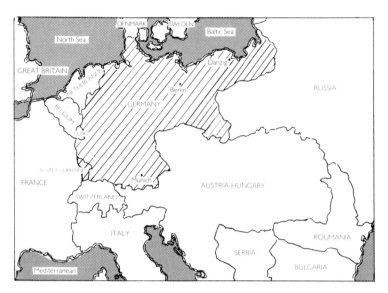

The boundaries of Germany before 1914.

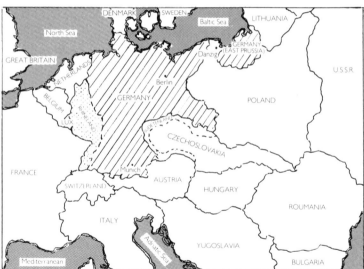

The frontiers of Germany after the Versailles settlement of 1919.

Czechoslovakia   The last weeks of the war had seen the collapse of the Austro-Hungarian Empire, and this had given the Czechs and Slovaks, who had long resented Austrian rule, a chance to form their own independent state of Czechoslovakia. The Versailles Treaty confirmed the legitimacy of the new republic and settled its frontiers.

Many Germans were angry that the new Czech state incorporated over three million German-speaking subjects of the former Austro-Hungarian Empire. Most of these now resented and despised their new rulers, but although they protested vehemently, they had no success in persuading the Allies to shift the frontier line to include them in the new Germany. These people became known as the Sudeten Germans, though in fact their homes were scattered all along the frontiers of the provinces of Bohemia and Moravia (i.e. Western Czechoslovakia), far away from the mountain range from which they took their name. After the initial protests the Sudetens seem to have accepted the new arrangement, but they were to provide a possible source of disaffection available to any future German government who wished to exploit their situation and make common cause with them against Czechoslovakia.

Austria
The Austrians themselves were thoroughly aggrieved by the clause in the settlement forbidding them from ever uniting with Germany in one state. Most Germans accepted this readily enough, but to many Austrians, it seemed yet one more blow to their hopes of rebuilding their position in Europe.

The Rhineland
The handing over to France of Alsace Lorraine, a former French province, was accepted by the new German republic with little protest. A more difficult matter was the arrangement imposed on the Rhineland, indisputably German territory lying mainly on the German side of the Rhine. The French, who had suffered particularly from having had a frontier with Germany, now wanted to make sure that the Rhineland was securely under their control – they believed this was the only way that they could be permanently guaranteed protection from German attack. The other Allies disagreed, and a compromise decision was reached. The Rhineland was to remain German, but was to be occupied by French and British troops until Germany had paid in full the reparations (enforced "compensation") imposed on her by the Treaty of Versailles. Even in 1925, when it was agreed by the Treaty of Locarno that the French and British troops should be withdrawn, Germany was still strictly forbidden to establish fortifications on the left bank of the Rhine or at any point that was within fifty kilometres of French territory. No German soldiers were to be stationed, and no military manoeuvres held there. So the Rhineland, though now unoccupied by foreign troops, was made a *demilitarized zone*; any attempt to re-establish German military control was to be regarded as an act of aggression and

would be dealt with by force. It was a telling reminder to the German people that although eight years had passed since their defeat, they were still not their own masters. The Rhineland became a symbol of continuing German impotence – another German grievance that, in the right circumstances, an ambitious nationalist politician might exploit in his favour.

The Polish question The Versailles settlement of the Polish question was hardest of all for German national pride to stomach. Ever since the end of the seventeenth century, the foreign policy of the two leading German states, Prussia and Austria, had centred on the task of acquiring more power and influence in Eastern Europe. Prussia, later to become the leading state of the new unified Germany, had been particularly determined to acquire more territory beyond her existing eastern frontier, partly for reasons of security, and partly in order to end the geographical separation of her territories. Because of the combined pressure, not only from Prussia and Austria, but also from Russia, the kingdom of Poland underwent three partitions and indeed disappeared altogether as a state in 1795.

Now, at Versailles, over a hundred years later, she was demanding recognition of her independence and the return of all her original land. This suited the Allies, not only because of the current sympathies with Polish aspirations, but because they believed that a strongly anti-German state on Germany's eastern borders would improve European security from future German threats.

The Commission on Polish Affairs at the peace conference therefore recommended that large areas of the German provinces of East and West Prussia, Pomerania, Posnania and Upper Silesia should be given up to Poland. Lloyd George, the British Prime Minister, had reservations about this, because he believed that the terms were unrealistically harsh, and that a humiliated Germany, with millions of her people living under Polish rule, would be unlikely to help the long-term stability of Europe.

The Danzig issue at He therefore insisted that the German port of Danzig,
Versailles originally to have been awarded to Poland, should instead be made a free city under the supervision of the League of Nations. He also proposed that the new frontiers should not be arbitrarily imposed, but that people living in areas where there was a mixture of nationalities, including Germans,

should be given the opportunity of voting in a plebiscite as to whether they preferred to live under Polish or German rule. Even so, after the voting was finally over, more than a million Germans found themselves living under an alien government. Moreover, Germans living in Germany found that their hard-won geographical unity had been destroyed: the Polish corridor, a strip of land giving Poland an outlet to the sea at Danzig, separated a large block of German territory (East Prussia) from the rest of the fatherland. Although Germans were given special rights of transport across the Polish Corridor, its creation was still a bitter blow.

German reactions to Versailles

Resentment about these territorial settlements was further fuelled by the decimation of Germany's once powerful armed forces, and the Allies' attempt to root out Germany's deeply entrenched militaristic tradition. The German army was reduced to 100,000 men, compulsory military training of young men was abolished, and private clubs were forbidden to train their members in the use of arms. The navy was reduced to only 6 battleships, 6 light cruisers, 12 destroyers and 12 torpedo boats. There were to be no submarines at all. In this way the Allies hoped to emasculate German militarism, and make Europe safe. It is, however, one thing to make a decree – quite another to enforce it. Germany was, after all, still an independent, sovereign nation. There was no occupying power to see that these conditions were carried out, and, as we shall see, it was to prove relatively easy for Germany to disregard the provisions of the Versailles settlement, once she had a leader bold enough to defy the rest of Europe.

Similarly, the policy of reparations agreed at Versailles could only be carried out with the full cooperation of Germany. The question was how far she should be made to pay for the destruction caused by the war. Germany had admitted that she had invaded Belgium, Luxembourg and France, but claimed that she had acted in self-defence and could not therefore be described as an aggressor. However, the clause dealing with reparations did indeed name Germany as an aggressor. Although their representatives had no choice but to sign the Versailles agreement, the German people were furious about this moral condemnation of them, as well as about the amount of money they were expected to pay. Reparations were to yield only limited rewards to the Allies, but the subject was to foment the most bitter resentment in Germany, providing a major source of trouble in the future.

Despite the country's deep economic troubles in the early post-war years, the policy of reparations did not have the crippling effect on Germany that some statesmen and economists had predicted. Furthermore, the original demands were whittled down over the years and Germany was able to finance her repayments with loans from the United States. Nevertheless, the original bitterness remained; reparations could always be blamed by the Germans for all their troubles, and served to remind them of the injustice of their situation.

The war had left Germany beaten and resentful, feeling impotent and frustrated, and knowing that the Allied European powers were ranged against her.

In the end, the impotence was to prove imagined rather than real. Despite all the efforts made at Versailles, Germany's economic and military potential, though dormant, remained tremendous. Moreover, Germany's indignation at the way in which she had been treated would give that military revival an especially dangerous and hostile character.

How did Hitler become so powerful in Germany?

German discontent Although the Germans had had no choice but to accept the terms of Versailles, there was a widespread conviction that they were grossly unjust, and a root cause of the serious economic troubles that beset Germany in the immediate post-war period. The resentment of the army, in particular, was encouraged by the much-quoted remark of an unidentified British general that the army had been "stabbed in the back" by Germany's own politicians. This implied that there had been no military reason for the German surrender and further confirmed the belief that the German defeat had not been deserved, and must never be accepted.

The democratic Weimar Republic, which had been set up as the new government of Germany to replace the Hohenzollern monarchy, was regarded by many disillusioned, conservative Germans as a puppet of Versailles, and therefore unworthy of either loyalty or respect. There was bitter enmity between such people, who remained obsessed by their fatherland's past glories, and those Germans who belonged to the trade unions and to the Social Democratic Party, and who supported their new, more enlightened government and looked forward to a greater measure of democracy.

The inauguration of the Weimar government.

It is important to remember that over this debate loomed the shadow not only of German defeat, but of the Russian Revolution that had begun in 1917. The events in Russia had demonstrated to the world that socialism was not just a political idea but a system of government that had toppled a monarchy and started to transform the social and economic fabric of a nation. Whether you agreed or disagreed with socialist principles like communal ownership of property, land and industry, abolition of the old social classes and increased recognition of the importance of ordinary workers, they could no longer be dismissed as impractical.

Bavaria The situation in Germany was further complicated by the political struggles going on in different parts of the country. The government in Berlin found Bavaria, a province in the south of Germany, especially difficult to deal with. The extreme left-wing government there, established at the end of the war, had been overturned, and parties devoted to the return of the Bavarian monarchy, and to the complete suppression of socialism and democracy, now held sway. This right-wing government was supported by many returning soldiers who had fought bravely for their country, and were now angry and disillusioned by the economic chaos and widespread unemployment that awaited them.

The emergence of Among these soldiers returning to Bavaria was Adolf Hitler,
Hitler a young Austrian, consumed with bitterness at the humiliation of both Austria and Germany, and already seeing Germany as the potential leader of a union of both countries. His zeal and opinions impressed his army superiors, and he was made an education officer, entrusted with the task of combating the new and, in the army's view, dangerous ideas of pacifism, socialism and democracy. Hitler's time as an instructor led him to an important discovery – that of his own capacity to speak fluently, loudly and powerfully.

However powerful his speeches, he still needed a political organization through which to make his views widely heard. In 1919 he joined the committee of the German Workers' Party, an organization which appealed to him because of its combination of right-wing ideas and working-class membership. By 1920, under his influence and eventual leadership, this tiny party had been transformed into a growing political force, and given a new name – the National Socialist German Workers' Party. The first four letters of the German for this name gave the term "Nazi".

More and more people at this time were frightened by the runaway inflation that was destabilizing the economy, and shocked by the French occupation in 1923 of the Ruhr, their industrial heartland, as a reprisal for non-payment of reparations. Dispirited by the crisis their country was enduring, they flocked to Hitler's meetings to hear the strong messages he was putting over with such an aggressively confident delivery. They warmed to his calls for a strong authoritarian central government, a repudiation of the Versailles settlement, and a greater and mightier Germany. They liked, too, the way he attacked Jews as a danger to society; it fitted in with the long tradition of Bavarian anti-Semitism, and gave them a convenient scapegoat for their anger and indignation.

The November Putsch

By November 1923, Hitler believed that the time was ripe for an attempt by his party and allied groups to take over political power in Munich, the Bavarian capital. He was confident that he would be unopposed, even supported by the Bavarian government, which was itself extremely right-wing and at odds with the national government in Berlin. However, he soon found he had miscalculated. His force of 3,000 S.A. storm-troopers – his "strong-arm" troops formed from willing

The young Hitler serving his sentence in Landsberg prison.

and enthusiastic servicemen – was stopped by the Bavarian police before reaching the War Ministry, and the attempted coup was put down firmly, with sixteen Nazis killed and many more wounded. Hitler was put on trial, but he turned the tables on his accusers and his eloquence won him some useful publicity. He was sentenced to five years in prison, but served less than nine months. Because of his notably lenient treatment, Hitler's time in prison gave him the leisure to develop further his beliefs about the future of the German-speaking peoples, and to formulate them in his book *Mein Kampf* (*My Struggle*).

Hitler had much to say in his book about the future of Germany as the founder of an empire of German-speaking people that would one day dominate Europe. He had also evolved firm ideas about national politics which included the need for unquestioning obedience and loyalty to the German state and nation, the duty of the government to impose an absolute authority on the people, the acceptance of force, even of brutality, as a necessary method of maintaining that authority, and the ruthless suppression of any opposition. These beliefs, together with hatred of the Jews and a passionate wish to preserve the purity of the German race, were the basis of Nazism. They are also called fascist, because their military-style authoritarianism had many points of similarity to the creed propounded by Benito Mussolini, who came to power as *Il Duce* (the leader) of Italy in 1922.

He, like Hitler, responded to the social and economic problems which beset his country in the immediate post-war years by advocating a totalitarian regime – that is, one of absolute authority. He adopted as an emblem for his movement the "fasces" – the bundle of rods with an axe in the middle that had been carried in processions through Ancient Rome, to proclaim to the people the power of the government of those days to use flogging and execution as legitimate instruments of its rule. This was the origin of the word "fascist" which was adopted by the political party which Mussolini founded, and was later applied to the Nazi Party and to similar movements in other countries.

Hitler's struggle for power   Hitler came out of prison full of determination to continue his struggle to convert the whole of Germany to Nazi ideas – only to find that his audience had almost disappeared. Aided by substantial American loans and by the softer attitude now being shown by other European countries, Germany at last seemed to be getting on her feet again. A less bitter public was less ready to listen to Hitler's outpouring of hatred or to his dreams of future glory. He refused to be discouraged. He was convinced that this period of economic and social calm could not last, and he was right.

His predictions were confirmed by the Wall Street Crash of 1929. Germany had borrowed heavily from the United States, and the American Depression had severe repercussions in Germany. The loans were eventually called in and consequently the winter of 1929-30 saw the level of German unemployment rise to 3,000,000.

Once again Hitler was able to exploit an economic situation that was exactly right for the ideas outlined in *Mein Kampf* to take root. His demands for more territory for German-speaking peoples, as well as his fierce denunciations of Jews and Communists, appealed to those Germans who were once again looking for a way out of their troubles.

Moreover, his party by now had two additional sources of strength: the paramilitary organization of storm-troopers, originally designed to protect Nazi speakers and which had by 1929 been so greatly extended that it formed a private army; and large donations of money from industrialists and businessmen who were prepared to support anyone who seemed likely to prevent a left-wing revolution.

Nevertheless, although the Nazi party had increased its representation in the German Parliament to the extent that in July 1932 it became the largest single party, its rise to power was not unchecked. Certainly the deepening economic crisis and the rise in unemployment did attract support for the Nazis both from ordinary voters and from other extreme right-wing groups, but there was also increasing support for the Communist Party, and at the November 1932 election the Nazis lost two million votes.

Large crowds gathered outside German savings banks as news of the financial crisis filtered through.

Hitler's support from the public grew again after Germany's economic troubles.

Indeed, despite the dramatic improvement in their fortunes since 1930, the Nazi party did not win more than 37% of the total vote in any free, properly run election. There would have been no chance of their coming to power if their political opponents had been willing to form a coalition against them.

However, the German right wing, which included the old ruling class, the army leaders, industrialists and businessmen, was not interested in cooperation to stop Hitler. They wanted to re-establish their own power over Germany at all costs, and were prepared to do a deal with Hitler in order to obtain the popular support, which he appeared to command, for their own policies. Accordingly, Schleicher, the German Chancellor, and von Papen, his predecessor, persuaded President Hindenburg of the wisdom of ensuring Hitler's cooperation and the votes of his followers by giving him the Chancellorship. Hindenburg, though doubtful, was anxious to secure a government that had a working majority and therefore some chance of ruling effectively, so freeing him from the necessity of ruling by personal decree. He wanted to see a more constitutional method of law-making.

The Chancellorship Consequently he allowed himself to be persuaded and on 30th January, 1933, Hitler was appointed Chancellor of Germany, as a price for his full cooperation.

Von Papen had been quite sure that once Hitler and his party had been absorbed into the government, they would be easily restrained from extreme actions and policies by their more experienced colleagues, especially as non-Nazis had a majority in the Cabinet. How wrong he was proved to be!

Hitler quickly and craftily secured an agreement for a fresh election should talks with the Centre Party, aimed at obtaining their cooperation, break down. Hitler made quite sure that those talks did fail, and the election that then followed was dominated not only by Hitler's speeches and ideas, but also by his bullying tactics. Opposing speakers were beaten, their posters torn down, and the newspapers supporting them were suppressed.

Although even then the Nazi party was to win only 45% of the votes, Hitler was able to push a new law through the *Reichstag* (Parliament) which gave him undisputed power whether he received a majority of votes or not. The trade unions, who continued to oppose him, were dissolved, anyone with a Jewish grandparent was excluded from political office, and Nazis were placed in all the most important government posts.

From then on Hitler can accurately be described as a dictator. Although he had the support at that time of scarcely half the public, he had made himself independent of any need for an electoral majority, and had learned to manipulate the political machinery to his own ends. Having securely established his power base, he could set about his self-appointed task of regenerating Germany's greatness.

Hitler reviews his storm-troopers in preparation for the general election of 1932.

How did Hitler become so powerful in Europe?

Hitler's policy in Europe

Having established his dictatorship, Hitler was now determined to establish German dominance in Europe. On 7th March, 1936, against the advice of his generals and with what he himself modestly described as "unshakeable obstinacy and amazing aplomb", he ordered German troops into the demilitarized zone of the Rhineland, which they had been strictly forbidden to enter. By treaty, the French were entitled to resist such an invasion by force – but they took no action. They and the British were at this time preoccupied with the situation in Abyssinia, which had recently been invaded by Mussolini, the dictator of Italy, and neither country felt that the German entry into the Rhineland was worth the risk of war. Hitler had taken a calculated gamble and got away with it. The German public went wild with triumph and gratitude, and at the subsequent "elections" held on 29th March they gave Hitler and his party (the only one tolerated) a 95% victory. The advice of the generals had been successfully ignored; so their position was weakened and Hitler's authority over them reinforced. He now felt even more confident that he could go ahead with his ambitious plans, with the army as well as the civilian public well under his spell.

German troops enter the demilitarized zone of the Rhineland.

On the first page of *Mein Kampf* Hitler had pronounced: "German Austria must return to the German Motherland." He saw this as a necessary first step to the realization of his dream of a German-speaking European empire which would give Germans the territory and opportunities he believed should rightfully be theirs. He was ready to deal summarily with any opposition to his scheme: "The soil exists," he said, again in *Mein Kampf*, "for the people which possesses the force to take it – what is refused to amicable methods, it is up to the fist to take."

He had great hopes that his planned take-over of Austria would be made easy by the efforts of the active Nazi party already thriving there. During 1934 these Austrian Nazis had kept up a widespread campaign of terrorism, blowing up public buildings and murdering supporters of the Austrian Chancellor, Engelbert Dollfuss, who was himself a ruthless dictator.

On 25th July, this campaign of terrorism reached a peak when 154 members of the Austrian Nazi party, dressed in Austrian army uniforms, broke into the Austrian Chancellery and shot Dollfuss in the throat. Other Nazis seized the radio station and broadcast reports of the Chancellor's resignation. However, Hitler's hopes of a speedy take-over were frustrated, firstly by the swift suppression of the rebellion by government forces under the direction of Kurt von Schuschnigg, the new Austrian Chancellor, and secondly by the threatening attitude taken up by Mussolini, the Italian *Duce* (leader). Having no wish to see German influence spread to a country on his own borders, he mobilized four of

The launching of Grafspee, *a sign of the re-emergence of German naval power.*

his divisions on the Brenner Pass. Mussolini intended the presence of these divisions to be a clear indication to Hitler that he was prepared to resist a German take-over of Austria, by military force if necessary.

For the moment Hitler had to accept defeat; but he was determined that the set-back should be only temporary. He realized that, to be sure of acting effectively, he must wait until his stealthy rebuilding of Germany's armed forces had given him the formidable military power with which to defy any opposition.

He decided that the German army should be increased from 100,000 to 300,000 by October 1934, and commissioned two battle cruisers, each of 20,000 tons – 16,000 tons above the limit allowed by the Versailles Treaty. He also ordered that a fleet of submarines should be secretly built.

The end of Versailles The secrecy did not prevent Britain and France from having some idea of what was going on, but they were in no mood to protest. Indeed, they were making proposals that Germany's right to rearm should be officially recognized. Encouraged by their conciliatory mood, Hitler took the risk of going further with his rearmament plans. He announced openly to the world that Germany now had an air force, and on 16th March, 1935, he introduced universal military service, so ensuring that he had a peace-time army of half a million men at his disposal.

This marked the overthrow of the Versailles settlement. Even those Germans who disapproved of Hitler's policies joined in the general rejoicing that the era of humiliation and defeat was over. Confident that he was now strong enough, Hitler once more began to look for the right moment to proceed with the annexation of Austria.

The Anschluss He was considerably helped by the fact that Schuschnigg was afraid of Germany's rapidly increasing military power, especially in view of the passivity of Britain and France. His fear for Austria's safety had led the Austrian Chancellor to seek an understanding with Hitler, and on 11th July, 1936, an agreement was concluded between Austria and Germany. Germany promised to respect Austria's sovereignty and independence; Austria promised that in matters of foreign policy she would always act in the interest of all Germans. In addition, there were several secret clauses by which Schuschnigg agreed to a major extension of Nazi influence within Austria.

41

Schuschnigg hoped that his acceptance of Hitler's demands would end the matter, and ease the tension between the two countries. However, this was not Hitler's way: he always met concessions not with softening, but with further demands.

In 1938, Schuschnigg, appalled by Hitler's pressure on Austria and evidence of continuing military preparations by Germany, decided to hold a plebiscite to ask the Austrians whether they were in favour of an independent Christian Austria. He hoped by this means to ensure a firm "No" to any extension of German influence. However, before the plebiscite could be held, a list of further demands from Hitler, together with a complete absence of support from Mussolini (now closely allied with the *Führer*), convinced Schuschnigg that the situation was hopeless. He resigned, and on 11th and 12th March, 1938, German troops marched over the border into Austria. In Vienna, the persecution of the Jewish community started immediately, with thousands of Jews imprisoned, deprived of their property and even made to scrub the pavements, surrounded by groups of jeering Nazis. Hitler's dream of the *Anschluss* – the union of Germany and Austria to form Greater Germany – was now a reality.

German forces enter Austria in triumph.

Czechoslovakia Emboldened by this success, Hitler turned to the next area that he had decided was to be an essential part of his new Third Reich – Czechoslovakia. Here again he knew there was a ready-made ally within the country – the German-speaking Sudetens who, after the Versailles settlement, had found themselves under the rule of an alien government. Their discontent had been increased by their poverty, as they were largely employed in the light industries which had been particularly badly hit by the worldwide economic depression.

On 20th May, 1938, the Czech government under President Beneš, aware that Czechoslovakia was now likely to become Hitler's next quarry, and alarmed by news of German troop movements near the frontier, decided to prepare for the worst by partially mobilizing their armed forces. This was interpreted by Hitler as a provocative act and he made sure that the greatest possible publicity was given to it and to the alleged sufferings of the Sudetens.

This time it was more difficult for Britain and France to remain aloof, because France was bound by treaty to come to the aid of Czechoslovakia if she were attacked. Nevertheless, both governments were determined to avoid war at all costs, and urged Beneš to be conciliatory towards Hitler and to make further concessions to the Sudetens.

Hitler receives the adulation of the Reichstag after the annexation of Austria.

Once again, Hitler followed the usual pattern and responded to these concessions with more peremptory demands. By September 1938 he had made it quite clear that

he would be satisfied with nothing less than the complete surrender of all Sudeten territory to Germany. The hectoring tone of his public speeches and official communications, together with the ruthlessness of his demands, shocked the people as well as the governments of the other European powers. They were also frightened, because Hitler had no hesitation in threatening to use force if his demands were not met, and this put his peace-loving opponents at a considerable disadvantage.

On 15th September, 1938, amid the deepening crisis, Neville Chamberlain, the British Prime Minister, flew to Germany to see if a personal meeting with Hitler would do anything to resolve the situation. He had already been briefed by the British ambassador in Berlin, Sir Nevile Henderson , who took the view that Hitler, despite his threats, was really quite reasonable, and certainly did not want war with Britain.

Chamberlain, desiring to keep the peace at almost any cost, was only too ready to believe Henderson's version of Hitler's intentions. Hitler himself, seeking to keep Britain neutral, talked to Chamberlain calmly and plausibly and managed to convince him that if Czechoslovakia would give up the Sudetenland, he would make no further demands and Europe could rest in peace. Chamberlain, together with the more reluctant Daladier, the French Premier, decided to trust the German leader and to persuade Beneš to do what Hitler asked.

The signatories of the Munich Agreement, 1938. On the right are Mussolini and Ciano, his foreign minister.

Hitler immediately responded to this retreat by his usual stepping-up of pressure. He protested that the transfer of power was not taking place quickly enough, and declared that, unless the Czechs cooperated, he would have no choice but to invade. The Czech reply to this blatant bullying was to mobilize once again, and to reject Hitler's demands as "absolutely and unconditionally unacceptable".

On 26th September Britain and France issued a joint communiqué proclaiming their intention of supporting the Czechs, and Europe trembled on the brink of war. Chamberlain approached Mussolini to see what he could do to calm the situation, and the Italian dictator managed to persuade Hitler to put off his invasion and to attend a four-power conference to settle the Czech dispute. Britain, France, Germany and Italy were to decide on the fate of the Czechs; the Czechs themselves were not to be invited; nor were the Russians, who were snubbed despite their declared willingness to cooperate with Britain and France in opposing German designs on Czechoslovakia.

All Europe seemed to be dancing to Hitler's tune. When Chamberlain, on 28th September, told a worried House of Commons that Hitler had agreed to a conference and that he had asked Chamberlain to fly out to Munich the following day, the Members of Parliament threw their order papers into the air like delighted schoolboys. Jan Mesaryk, the Czech ambassador to London, looked down on the scene from the

Chamberlain returns to Croydon Airport with "peace in our time".

gallery, hardly able to believe the clear signs that his country was about to be deserted.

His worst fears were realized as the four powers, meeting the following day, agreed that the Sudeten territory should be completely evacuated by the Czechs before 10th October. The final determination of boundaries was to be agreed by a five-power commission, and Britain and France bound themselves to guarantee the sovereignty of Czechoslovakia in her reduced form and to come to her aid in case of attack.

Chamberlain returned home to scenes of wild rejoicing, claiming that he had secured "peace in our time". The Czechs were left to face a stunning diplomatic defeat and the knowledge that their territory, shorn of its protective mountains and the industrialized Sudetenland, was now wide open to German attack. Understandably, they put little faith in the Franco-British guarantee.

Their scepticism was proved well-founded when Hitler, on 15th March, 1939, proclaimed himself thoroughly dissatisfied with the Munich agreement, and gave the order for German forces to march into Czechoslovakia. Britain and France were able to wriggle out of their promise to come to Czecho-slovakia's aid because by this time the Slovaks, one of the peoples who made up the Czech state, had withdrawn, with German encouragement, to set up their own independent state. The two allies were thus able to argue that the frontiers they had promised to defend no longer existed and there was "internal disruption" in the state they had pledged themselves to guarantee.

By now, supremely confident of his power, unopposed and unmatched by any other European statesman, Hitler seemed to himself and to millions of other people to be destined to become the absolute master of Europe.

Why did no one stop him?

In Germany   There were many groups and individuals in Germany who disapproved of Hitler from the very outset of his career. Some were willing to speak out; others chose to keep quiet. Two important factors damped down the sparks of rebellion. Firstly there was the irresistibility of a leader and programme offering rescue from demoralization and depression; secondly there was the degree to which Germans had grown used over the past two hundred years to a foreign policy that was geared to the acquisition of new territory in Europe. In this respect, Hitler was preaching nothing new and it was therefore easy for the German public to accept his ideas.

This meant that the task of the opposition groups was discouragingly hard, and it was made even harder, after Hitler's rise to power in 1933, by the efficient machinery of censorship and repression that was a characteristic of his regime. Fear of torture, imprisonment and death is a powerful argument against speaking out.

The German trade union movement did speak out in opposition to Hitler's policies during the 1920s and early '30s, but when Hitler became Chancellor, they decided to try to work with the new government. In 1933 they came in all good faith to the National Labour Day organized by the new Nazi government. Trade union members hoped that this was a gesture of goodwill and they cooperated with enthusiasm – only to find that the gathering was used as an opportunity for Hitler to occupy all trade union headquarters, confiscate the unions' funds, and arrest many of their leaders, even those who had protested their friendship and support for his regime. So ended any hope of effective opposition from the trade unions.

Hitler's storm-troopers guard prisoners suspected of hostility to his regime. The brutality of the Nazi regime made opposition difficult.

The Communist Party was hostile to Nazism, and frequently embroiled in fights and brawls at Nazi meetings. But it refused to cooperate with other anti-Nazi groups, either to prevent Hitler's rise to power or to overthrow him once his regime was established. The Communists rather believed that their first task was to overthrow the power of the middle classes and Social Democrats, and that Hitler's regime, if left to itself, would inevitably collapse, so leaving a power vacuum which they, the Communists, would fill.

The Social Democratic Party itself was confused and dispirited, lacking the decisiveness to challenge Hitler effectively. They took refuge in compromise with the Nazi government, but little good it did them: their party, declared "subversive and inimical to the state", was dissolved.

Both the Catholic and the Protestant churches at first tried to cooperate with Hitler. Many Protestants especially had welcomed the new emerging strength of Germany. They were, after all, still deeply influenced by the ideas of Martin Luther, their sixteenth-century founder, who had taught absolute obedience to the state and had been strongly anti-semitic. Even Pastor Niemöller, later imprisoned in Dachau, the infamous concentration camp, at first saw Hitler's rise to power as a healthy sign of national revival. It was only when both denominations experienced the distasteful effects of Hitler's policies that they began, often with great courage, to oppose him.

The most significant challenge to Hitler came secretly. Many of the leading army generals had from the beginning been unhappy about Hitler's methods and some had openly challenged the brutality of the storm-troopers. By 1937 there

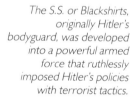

The S.S. or Blackshirts, originally Hitler's bodyguard, was developed into a powerful armed force that ruthlessly imposed Hitler's policies with terrorist tactics.

were also growing doubts in army quarters about the wisdom of Hitler's foreign policy. The Chief of the General Staff, General Beck, tried to organize his brother generals to make a stand against Hitler, but his plan collapsed and the reasons for his subsequent resignation were never allowed to reach the German public.

He did, however, in retirement, continue to plan Hitler's overthrow, aided by three other generals – von Witzleben, von Brockdorff-Ahlefeld and Hoepner, all of whom held important commands. These military figures were supported by a distinguished group of civilians including Carl Goerdeler, the Mayor of Leipzig, 1930-7, Ulrich von Hassell, the German ambassador in Rome, and Johannes Popitz, the Prussian Minister of Finance. They all acknowledged that the one hope of getting rid of Hitler rested with the army, which alone would have access to the necessary force.

Their plan was to wait for Hitler's announcement of the invasion of Czechoslovakia, timed, as they knew, for 1st October, 1938, and then to arrest him and take him before one of the people's courts, charged with involving his people in an unnecessary war. They were quite sure, when they drew up their plan, that Hitler's march on the Czechs would inevitably lead to an immediate declaration of war by Britain and France.

Chamberlain's flight to Munich and Hitler's postponement

General Beck, whose attempt to overthrow Hitler was frustrated.

of the invasion threw them into disarray, and the plan was called off. Whether the plan would have succeeded if Britain and France had played their expected part is open to question. Certainly there is evidence to show that there was no great public support for Hitler's invasion and with concerted resistance from the army, as well as from his other opponents, he could have been in a vulnerable position. As it was, his enemies were disunited and therefore impotent to challenge his deeply entrenched regime.

In Britain By the time Hitler came to power, most British politicians regretted the vengeful attitude towards Germany that had dominated the Versailles Conference. The costs of the 1914-18 war in human and financial terms had been terrible, and there was a strong desire for peace among politicians of all three parties. Consequently, Britain was an enthusiastic supporter of the Locarno Treaty of 1925, which was designed to modify the harsher provisions of the Versailles Treaty and to usher in an era of peace and stability in which Germany would be accorded full recognition as a European power. A conscious effort was made in the years following Locarno to become more friendly with Germany, and to persuade France to settle her differences with her former enemy.

Even before Hitler came to power, Germany was demanding the right to rearm. The German representatives at the 1932 Disarmament Conference called by the League of Nations made it very clear that if Germany were to cooperate in the reduction of armaments, she must first be allowed an equal right to arm herself.

The British Prime Minister at the time was Ramsay MacDonald who, in his idealistic vision of a peaceful Europe, was disposed to be conciliatory towards Germany's demands. The succeeding Conservative Prime Minister, Stanley Baldwin, was equally pacific in his attitude, even when Hitler's advent had made clear Germany's uncompromisingly aggressive outlook.

There were politicians who disagreed with this policy of appeasement. Sir Robert Vansittart, the Permanent Under-Secretary of State for Foreign Affairs, was convinced that Germany would "loose off another European war just as soon as it feels strong enough". Winston Churchill, once a senior Conservative politician but relegated to the back benches between 1929 and 1939, led a group of like-minded colleagues who warned continually against the dangers of coming to terms with Nazi Germany. The warnings were not taken seriously. Churchill's pleas for active rearmament in response to Hitler's stealthy build-up of forces, and for a strong anti-German alliance, to include Soviet Russia, were dismissed as pessimistic and misguided.

On this issue, most people of all parties preferred to support the Prime Minister, Stanley Baldwin, who had assured the public: "I give you my word that there will be no great armament." Politicians knew that this was the message that the voters wished to hear and, indeed, many of them sincerely believed that it was the only sensible policy. It seemed that rational men could not understand the mind of an irrational leader, or accept the fact that anyone responsible for the government of his country could possibly contemplate the use of force not as a last resort but as an acceptable means of imposing his policies on Europe.

Some people in influential positions even had a sneaking admiration for Hitler's achievements and, in particular, for his hostility towards the Communist regime of Soviet Russia.

Hitler knew how to cultivate a warm and likable image. A smiling, "fatherly" Hitler chats to a young member of the Hitler Youth, the Nazi organization for young people.

STILL HOPE

Chamberlain's attempts at appeasement commanded genuine admiration from many of the public, as this cartoon from Punch, *21st September, 1938, suggests.*

Others actually espoused Hitler's ideas. Sir Oswald Mosley formed his own British Union of Fascists as early as 1932. Politicians and statesmen who visited Hitler in the post-war years included many who, though not formerly sympathetic to his ideas, admired the way in which he had overcome the Depression in Germany and had made the country respected again. They were completely taken in by his friendly manner and his soothing reassurances; their own wish for peace made them easy targets for Hitler's expert propaganda.

Many politicians and diplomats, moreover, including Sir Nevile Henderson, had the uneasy conviction that Hitler's claims in Europe were understandable, even justifiable. Their uncertainty about the issues seemed to blind them to the bullying tone and the threats of force which in themselves should have given sufficient cause for firm and united action.

As it became increasingly clear that reassurance and conciliation were not going to pacify Hitler, the protests from Churchill and his group grew louder. But those who were wedded to appeasement, though recognizing the danger, still clung to a policy of maintaining peace at all costs. The wish to make peace was replaced by a feverish effort to avoid war, and this made the British government quite incapable of standing up to Hitler during the time when firmness had a chance of being effective.

In France Having suffered so greatly in the 1914-18 war, and with Germany so close a neighbour, France in the immediate post-war years was implacably opposed to any softening in Western Europe's attitude to Germany.

From 1933, however, France was divided. The left wing opposed everything Hitler stood for, whereas many industrialists and right-wing politicians were impressed by the achievements of fascism. During the 1930s the hostility between the right and left wings of French politics grew so bitter that the French government was enfeebled for dealing with international affairs. Because of this, French influence in Europe was greatly weakened, and it was further decreased in 1935 when the Saar, the industrial region of Germany confiscated at Versailles and controlled by France, was returned to Germany by the League of Nations, after a plebiscite. The results of this had been materially influenced by Goebbels' propaganda and his donation to the Saarlanders of thousands of free radio sets.

In the same year, in response to the obvious growth of German military power, Paul Reynaud, a radical member of the French Parliament, urged that French military service should be extended to two years. This would improve the quality of the French army, which would inevitably be out-numbered in time by that of Germany, with her much larger population. Like Churchill in Britain, he was dismissed as an alarmist and his message was ignored.

The crucial point at which a more resolute French government could have stopped Hitler was the German reoccupation of the demilitarized zone of the Rhineland. Their entitlement to use force against Germany was clear, but the cabinet was divided, and preoccupied with Mussolini's aggression in Abyssinia. The French generals were unwilling to act, and France's British allies were equally reluctant. So Hitler's daring decision was left unpunished.

France's internal divisions were deepened by the outbreak of the Spanish Civil War. Most of the right-wing politicians sympathized with General Franco, who was fighting to overthrow the lawfully established left-wing government of Spain. Germany and Italy both supported Franco with men and materials; pilots and planes of the German Condor Legion were responsible for one of the most notorious episodes of the Civil War, the destruction of the village of Guernica. By contrast, France and Britain did nothing to help Spanish democracy. The French left wing, which supported the Spanish government and was urging French military intervention, was accused by its political opponents of risking the peace of France to aid a Communist revolution.

Even the left wing itself was split: a number of them, though sympathetic to the Spanish Republicans and hostile to Hitler, were nevertheless pacifists who believed that military force must always be avoided. In Spain as well as in the rest of Europe, fascism continued its seemingly irresistible advance.

Although France began from 1937 to build up her armed forces and to strengthen her fortifications against Germany with the impressive Maginot Line (a system of elaborate defences, mostly underground, along her north-east frontier), like Britain she lacked the political unity or the will to build up a realistic response to the danger that threatened across her border.

Mussolini Although he too was a fascist dictator, Mussolini did not automatically support Hitler, and as we have seen in the matter of Austria, his opposition could be very effective. However, from 1934 onwards, Mussolini busied himself with the conquest of Abyssinia, and his military plans were clearly dependent on reliable supplies of German coal which he needed to fuel the trains and ships in which his armies and equipment were transported.

Consequently, the two countries moved closer together and on 1st November, 1936, Mussolini referred to the relationship between Berlin and Rome as "an axis around which can revolve all those European states with a will to collaboration and peace". The relationship between the two countries, although undefined by any formal agreement, was referred to from then on as the Rome-Berlin Axis and it was accepted by both countries as the pivot of fascism. Mussolini's power to inhibit Hitler's plans in Europe was thus effectively neutralized.

The League of Nations

To many hopeful people, the League of Nations, set up at the end of the war to provide an organization to which all nations of the world could belong, offered the way forward to guaranteed peace. The League was to assume responsibility for administering disputed territories, organizing international cooperation, arbitrating in international quarrels and dealing with aggression.

Its effectiveness, however, was weakened at the outset by the refusal of the United States to become a member, and by the initial exclusion of Soviet Russia and Germany. Although Germany was admitted in 1926, she withdrew again in 1933, after Hitler took power.

Weakened by the absence of those three powerful states, the League was too dependent on goodwill and voluntary submission to its rulings, to be truly effective in establishing itself as a world authority. The emphasis placed by its constitution on the necessity for the freest possible discussion made it an organization ill-suited for action. As, one by one, the smaller states in the world found the League unable to protect them against fascism, either by economic sanctions or by military support, they turned in desperation to the larger powers for help.

With the League of Nations shown to be impotent in the face of such events as the Japanese invasion of Manchuria in 1931 and Italy's attack on Abyssinia in 1936, smaller nations like Czechoslovakia and far-sighted politicians in all countries could see that the only bastion left against Hitler's Germany was a strong defensive alliance of the other great European powers, Britain, France and Soviet Russia. All of them were threatened by Hitler's plans and all had considerable resources which combined might have proved an awe-inspiring deterrent even to him. But, as we shall see in the next chapter, that alliance, although suggested, was never achieved, and Hitler proceeded with his ruthless policy unchecked. By the time his bluff was called, it was too late to avoid a confrontation.

Why Poland?

We have seen how Hitler's ruthlessness, combined with the appeasing policies of both Britain and France, left Austria and Czechoslovakia hopelessly unprotected. Why was it that those policies were reversed, and why did the consequent head-on confrontation take place over Poland?

The end of appeasement

As we have seen, there had always been a measure of opposition to the policy of appeasement in Britain and France. Once German troops had marched into Czechoslovakia in March 1939, public opinion, no longer able to go on hoping for the best, began to swing behind those politicians who advocated a tough stand against Hitler. There was no significant German minority in what remained of Czechoslovakia, to justify Hitler's invasion.

Even Chamberlain's attitude began to harden, partly because of his own disillusionment, partly, perhaps, because his political antennae could sense the shift in the attitude of the electorate. In his speeches he still defended the Munich settlement, but sounded increasingly determined to resist "any attempt to dominate the world by force". His attitude was paralleled by that of Daladier, who was similarly supported by a newly resolute French public.

On 27th April, 1939, a limited measure of military service was introduced in Britain and in the same month the government began to explore the possibility, long advocated by Churchill, of a defensive alliance between Britain, France, Poland and Russia. The spur to this negotiation was the fear that Hitler would seize yet more territory in Eastern Europe. Perhaps this time it might be Poland, whose control over Danzig so infuriated Hitler; perhaps Soviet Russia, whose Communist ideology was so abhorrent to him; perhaps Romania, whose foreign minister was expressing fears of imminent German invasion. The British government proposed that Britain, together with France, Poland and Russia, should make an immediate declaration of her intention to resist any action "constituting a threat to the political independence of any European state".

One of the main factors in the ultimate failure of this plan was the prevarication of Poland. The Polish Prime Minister Joseph Beck had an unrealistic idea of his country's military capability, and an unfortunate tendency to try to play off

Soviet Russia and Germany against each other. Even at this point, when the seriousness of the European situation was clear, not only to politicians but to everyone, Beck persisted in his belief that Hitler might still be amenable to diplomacy, and he suggested, rather than the four-power alliance, an Anglo-Polish agreement guaranteeing assistance to both Poland and Romania.

After long discussions with the cabinet and with the French Prime Minister, Chamberlain decided to agree to this proposal, and the French promised a similar guarantee. On 31st March, 1939, Chamberlain reported to the Commons the news of this historic decision. "I now have to inform the House," he said, "that . . . in the event of any action which clearly threatened Polish independence, and which the Polish Government accordingly considered it vital to resist with their national forces, His Majesty's Government would feel themselves bound at once to lend the Polish Government all support in their power. They have given the Polish Government all assurance to this effect. I may add that the French Government have authorised me to make it plain that they stand in the same position in this matter as do His Majesty's Government."

British policy, which had for so long tried to avoid entanglement in the defence of Europe, was reversed. Having missed any chance of obstructing Hitler which might have been successful, Britain was now committed to go to war on behalf of a country whose actions she had little hope of influencing, and for whom there was little possibility of doing anything practical. Chamberlain and Halifax, however, were quite convinced that such an arrangement was essential, if only to stop Poland allying herself with Germany in a desperate attempt to secure her own safety.

They were quite prepared to accept Beck's insistence that Soviet Russia should be excluded from the agreement. This was partly because of their anti-Communist outlook and partly because they believed that Russia's ideological hostility towards Germany would ensure her cooperation with Britain and France, even without the promise of a formal guarantee of her safety. Once the guarantee had been given to Poland, however, Britain and France found themselves in a situation of increasing danger and complexity.

Britain and France in difficulties The issue of Danzig was particularly difficult for them, because although they had both promised to defend Poland, they were aware that the rights and wrongs of this particular affair were not clear-cut. Here was a city, once German, with a predominantly German population, which wanted to return to the Reich and yet was prevented from doing so. It was easy to see the case for German reoccupation.

Certainly the guarantee did not have the hoped-for deterrent effect on Hitler. Despite his many public declarations of his desire for peace, he multiplied his threats and demands over the question of Danzig. He remained convinced that despite the novel firmness of Britain and France, they would once again back down rather than fight. Moreover, he regarded any suggestion that the stand of Britain and France had achieved a moderation in his attitude as a personal insult.

Chamberlain and Halifax did indeed devote all their efforts to the task of finding a way out. Great pressure was put on Beck to negotiate with Hitler, but the Poles proved to be difficult allies, overrating their own military and diplomatic strength and underestimating the seriousness of their situation.

The reluctant approach to Russia

As the danger of the British and French position became apparent, pressure grew from back-bench spokesmen for a more serious attempt at agreement with Russia. Chamberlain was still hesitant, but agreed to explore the possibility once again. Negotiations with Russia once more got under way but were desultory and long-drawn-out. Britain wanted moral support from Russia against Hitler, whereas Russia wanted a proper treaty of mutual assistance with the U.K. and France, as well as precise arrangements for action if any of her neighbours were threatened by German aggression.

The British could not agree to such a commitment, even in

Ribbentrop and Stalin shake hands after concluding the Soviet/German pact.

Hitler's meetings with Colonel Beck, the Polish foreign minister, failed to achieve any agreement.

order to suppress Nazism. There was a further difficulty that also held up the negotiations: the reluctance of Poland to agree to Russian access to her territory even if this proved necessary to her defence.

The non-aggression pact between Germany and Russia

As the arguing dragged on, Stalin and Molotov, the Foreign Minister, became more impatient. Their primary objective was self-protection for Russia. The possibility of an alliance with Germany became increasingly attractive to them. Subordinate officials of Russia and Germany had already been discussing such a possibility at the same time as the negotiations with Britain and France had been taking place. Suddenly, Hitler, well aware of the opportunity afforded by the stalemate between Russia and the West, stepped in and seized the chance of using the situation to Germany's advantage. Ribbentrop was ordered to Moscow forthwith. Molotov put forward the notion of a "non-aggression pact" (an agreement that neither country would attack the other, in any circumstances). The Germans agreed within twenty-four hours and although many details still remained to be settled, by 23rd August the pact was concluded and signed. The British and French were left with nothing, while Hitler was now quite secure in the knowledge that, if he did decide to invade Poland, he would be unimpeded by Russian intervention.

The final attempt to avoid war

Negotiations between Britain, France and Germany over the Danzig question now reached fever pitch, with the two Western allies putting every pressure possible on Poland to adopt a more conciliatory attitude – and failing. On 29th August Hitler suddenly seemed to weaken and announced that he was prepared to negotiate with Poland directly, if Poland would agree to send a representative with full powers (a plenipotentiary) to arrange a speedy resolution of the dispute. However, this plenipotentiary must arrive in Berlin the following day.

The French urged Beck to get to Berlin at once. The British were more cautious, even delaying their passing on of Hitler's message to Poland until 12.25 a.m. on 31st August. In any case, Beck was quite intransigent and refused to accede to Hitler's request that a plenipotentiary should be sent. He and Lipski, the Polish ambassador in Berlin, were quite sure that Hitler was finally weakening and that his regime was about to crack.

We cannot know for certain whether Hitler was genuine in his offer to negotiate, or whether it was merely a trick to deflect the world's attention while he prepared and completed the invasion of Poland. Whatever the truth of the matter, Poland seems to have been doomed to be the location of the outbreak of war. Her own determination to stand out against any negotiation, and the absence of any powerful, deterrent military alliance against Germany, made the march on Poland inevitable; and British and French guarantees ensured that the German attack was bound to flare up into a European war.

Unmechanized Polish troops could not back up Polish foreign policy effectively.

A day that made history?

For the people of Britain, France, Poland and Germany, 3rd September was certainly a day to remember. War began to disrupt the pattern of everyday existence, and people had to face the prospect of mass destruction and personal suffering.

Millions of others, living in countries as yet unaffected by the day's events, would also, by the end of the war in 1945, have seen their lives turned upside down by its consequences. For 3rd September proved to be the first day of a war that was to affect the whole world, and to affect its future history – often in completely unexpected ways.

The war stemmed from the aggressive bid of Nazi Germany to dominate her neighbours and to found a new empire of German-speaking peoples. Yet, by the end, Germany was occupied by four foreign powers and was to emerge from that occupation split into two separate states – the Federal Republic of West Germany and the Democratic Republic of East Germany. So much for Hitler's dream!

Britain and France had hoped, by taking a stand against Hitler, to defend the stability of Europe. But although they ended up on the winning side, and Hitler was defeated, Europe's economy was shattered, many of its cities were in ruins, and its countries aligned with the two blocs into which the continent was now divided – the Communist East and the "democratic", "capitalist" West.

In its early days the war was seen primarily as a European war, despite the involvement of the British Commonwealth. Yet in the course of the next five and a half years of unprecedentedly mobile warfare, the tide of bombardment, invasion and destruction engulfed not only Western Europe, but also Soviet Russia, North Africa, Asia (including China and Japan), the people if not the land of the United States, and the oceans of the whole world!

Moreover, the invention of the atomic bomb, and its use at Hiroshima and Nagasaki in 1945, introduced human beings to a kind of warfare that could not only eliminate their enemies but wipe out their whole species.

In terms of international policies, also, the world was transformed in ways unpredicted by the statesmen of September 1939. Most significant of these was the emergence of the superpowers – the United States and the U.S.S.R. – with their rival ideologies and their struggle for influence over world events. The United Nations inaugurated in 1945, was a manifestation of the world's enduring wish for peace, but it has not succeeded in eliminating the new tensions and anxieties that have replaced those that preoccupied Europe in 1939.

There were more positive results. Some of the inventions and discoveries designed to solve military problems had great universal value. The need to prevent the wounds of servicemen from becoming infected led to the eventual discovery of the way to manufacture penicillin in sufficient quantities. The effectiveness of penicillin had already been established by Alexander Fleming, but the new breakthrough by Sir Howard Florey meant that the medicine could now be made generally available. Such a reasonably cheap and effective drug, originally designed to benefit soldiers, sailors and airmen, was to transform the health of people all over the world. Similarly, new plastic surgery techniques were developed, prompted by the need to treat the appalling burns that were a feature of the war in the air. The wartime discoveries of radar and the jet engine led to improvements in transport.

Positive results came, too, from the fact that governments had to learn to plan their war effort efficiently and to maintain the health of the people from whom the armed forces were drawn. Governments became more used to taking responsibility for social conditions. The need to mobilize their resources to their utmost produced a new level of expertise in organization and administration. Moreover, as the war progressed, it became more important to organize on an international scale, since military campaigns involved increasing liaison and cooperation between different countries.

The lessons learned during the war sparked off by the events of 3rd September have, in some measure, helped us to repair the terrible destruction it caused. It remains to be seen whether we have learned enough to avoid a repetition.

Further reading

THE EVENTS

Sidney Aster, *The Making of the Second World War*, André Deutsch, 1973

Richard Broad & Suzie Fleming, *Nella's Last War*, Falling Wall Press, 1981

Angus Calder, *The People's War. Britain 1939-45*, Jonathan Cape, 1969 (Panther, 1979)

Robert Rhodes-James (ed), *Chips: The Diaries of Sir Henry Channon*, Weidenfeld & Nicolson, 1967

Tom Harrisson & Charles Madge, *War Begins at Home*, Chatto & Windus, 1940

Tom Harrisson & Charles Madge, *Chatto & Windus, 1940*

Liddell Hart, History of the Second World War, Cassell, 1970

Norman Longmate, *The Home Front*, Chatto & Windus, 1981

R.J. Minney, *The Private Papers of Hore Belisha*, Collins, 1960

E.S. Turner, *The Phoney War on the Home Front*, Michael Joseph, 1961

THE INVESTIGATION

Alan Bullock, *Hitler: a Study in Tyranny*, Pelican, 1962

Winston Churchill, *The Gathering Storm, The Second World War* Vol II, Cassell, 1948 (Pelican, 1986)

William Kimber (ed), *Memoirs of Field Marshal Keitel*, William Kimber, 1965

Roger Parkinson, *The Origins of World War Two*, Wayland, 1970

William L. Shirer, *The Rise and Fall of the Third Reich*, Secker & Warburg, 1960 (Pan Books, 1968)

A.J.P. Taylor, *English History 1914-1945*, OUP, 1965 (Penguin, 1981)

A.J.P. Taylor, *Origins of the Second World War*, Hamish Hamilton, 1963

Index